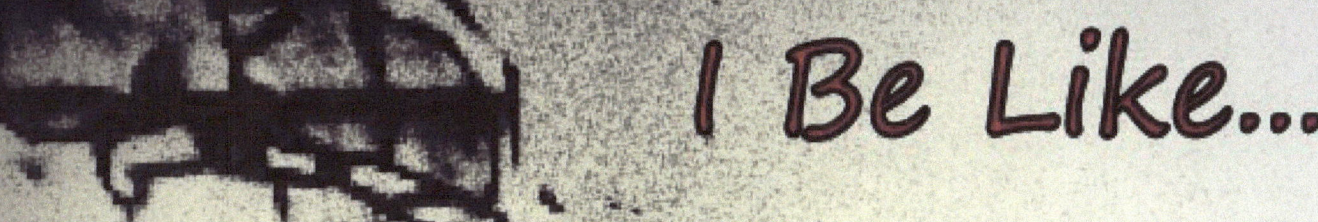

The Ingredients

Serving Size: 100%
Servings Per Magazine: 100%

ARTIST OF THE SUMMER - **BILLY BANG**
MODEL/OWNER OF B.Y.O.B - **NIKKI M**
HOOD LEGEND - **LEFRAK CITY, QUEENS**

ANTHONY 'BILLY BANG' CLARK

And many other unsigned artist including the youngest to be a part of the I-M-E family

Candice Jay	CClass Ave.
John Pritchett	Billy Bang
Olivia Gilmore	Felipe Sin
Steph Stone	& Chase Money
T-Ant	

Daily Value (DV) not commercial
Percent daily values (DV) are based on intellectual consumption.

Created and published by:
IME :: Invincible Marketing & Entertainment.
I Am Me :: I Make Entinties

UNSIGNED ARTIST // HOOD LEGENDS // MODELS // BUSINESS BUILDING // PROMOTING +MORE

OFHO-SHO HYPE
MAGAZINE
ISSUE #1

ARTIST OF THE SUMMER
BILLY BANG
UNSIGNED ARTIST
HOOD LEGEND
MODELS
BUSINESS BUILDING
PROMOTION
& MORE

serious GRAPHICS

NIKKI M. PAGE 17

WWW.OFHO-SHOHYPE.COM

"Hip Hop was set out in the dark,
they used to do it in the park"

- MC Shan

PHOTOS BY: DANTE

CHASE MONEY KRACKZ

"You can always chase money in Harlem"

ChaseMoney Krackz aka ChaseMoney or as I would prefer Esau Junior a College Grad has introduced his self to the world April 12th, 1992 in Harlem, NY. Named after his late father, Esau Champaigne Jr. dedicates all his hard work to his pop that passed away Sept 13, 1993.

Sitting down with this young man I learned quite a lot about what inspires him to do what he does and as most artists, it is the influence of life experiences that helped form and shape ChaseMoney into an entertainer in the music business. When asked what motivates his aura he replied, "As an entertainer I always want to keep it original and official. I'm not portraying anyone. I'm from Harlem, NY and there are a lot of things that go on in these streets that the media doesn't touch base on. I'm addressing it in my music. Also, the sense of hopelessness drives me to rap and find a way out the hood."

Most artists find a common ground and relate though that but with ChaseMoney, I find a very big difference in the way his music is transferred to the world compared to others. When looking into Esau' music I found that he is not much of an aggressor on the mic, but he makes valid points and notions that stand out. What I find most intriguing is that he also raps without a constant usage of profanity, not your average I must say.

In the years to come ChaseMoney plans to be around still moving along the entertainment field, but if that were to fail for him, he wants to be sure he gets himself into something that he loves doing and enjoys, by all means, a young man with such potential should want to be involved in something he adores.

Musically if he could work with anyone he chose to want to work with artists such as; Timberland, Pharrell and Missy the game in his eye and I must agree as well. He opted on those three producers because he idolized and admired them as a youth. ChaseMoney also wanted to add in that the R&B artist most likely chosen to work with would have to be Beyoncé or Alicia Keys and as an up and coming publicist, I love his choice of individuals!

Currently to date Chase Money has performed at a few different venues such as the "Cease The Violence" concert at the Jamaica Performance Center located in Queens, NY, Club Allure hosted by Def Jam A&R Shampoo and the Onyx lounge in Queens, NY just to name a few. He has two albums available on download on datpiff.com as well as a feature in the HARLEM CYPHER hosted by KSHARK TV found on youtube. ChaseMoney is definitely claiming the name and making himself known and I am honored to be able to help with that!

Suggestions of music I like from ChaseMoney and my number one choice pick is "Morning" off of his new mix tape entitled 'Big Money, Big Dreams'. I love this track because of the reggae melody in the hook and the beat alone is just smooth, it's definitely a song I like to replay! Another song suggestion is the song "Harlem", the beat is like a video game almost yet nice and party like, just the right song to ride to. Take my word for it when I say this kid here has a lot of potential and he's really just getting started!

If you want a sample of what he's about don't forget to check out KSHARK TV featured on youtube, the Harlem Cypher, something you don't want to miss. Also take your time to download his latest album 'Big Money, Big Dreams' found on datpiff.com.
StaarPower Ent.
www.soundcloud.con/Esau-junior

T.ANT
"THE CLEASNING"

T. Ant an up and coming Producer, Engineer and Artist hailing from Knoxville Tn.
"MUSIC IS MY PASSION!!"

Emerging from the same state as the daredevil Johnny Knoxville and the worlds most loved "hottie" Justin Timberlake, Anthony Clark formally known to others as T.Ant is rising to a plateau of higher elevation when he brings to light the underground artists that help to make music what it was while working on his own form of music.

When asked what inspires his drive for what he does, this young man stated that he has found himself in a world that triggers his most creative thoughts for what he loves, music!! What makes him a stand-out kind of guy is the fact that not only does he make his own music he also writes, produces and engineers his work as well which gives him the opportunity to "tailor" his soundtrack of life the way he would see fit.

Currently to date he has created 3 albums titled 'BusyLazyDayz', 'TBA and 'The Cleansing'. If you want to know why I chose to write on this artist you're going to have to check out his work!! What I will say is that the flow and vibe of these albums to me is that of Andre 3000, Common and other unique artists; thus saying that his flow his melodic, yet a smooth kind of rap that anyone can appreciate.

I had to wonder with such a unique blend of music, who would this young man like to get in the studio with and his reply was, "Kanye West, Jay-Z and Kendrick Lamar. Nice line up I must say.

Do you compare yourself to anyone in the industry, "NO! I'm me!!" stated T.Ant firmly and secure.

T.Ant shows most of his efforts establishing foundations for other unsigned artists such as Taylor Brandon also hailing from Tennessee. Tracks from this artist like 'Love Stop' and 'Until Then' are tracks that I thought intrigued me most.

"While being inspired by many of the greats, I hope to carry on the tradition of creating beautiful music. My project "Darkness: The Cleansing" could be described as "Trill Life, Dope View" filled with original sounds that mold the story of her, me, them, and us; 'darkness" gives a realistic but common view of me, more than just a hope of stardom, this is the story of me."

In the years to come, T.Ant looks to continue building his brand by bringing his production company to a larger existence. He chooses to continue in the music industry writing music and becoming a music critic in which I think and strongly believe we need that in this new society of music. So be on the look-out for what this multi-player in the game has in store. He's going to make a mark, BELIEVE DAT!!

Put The "R" Back in R&B, Please!

Olivia Gilmore, born April 11, was raised in Hollis, Queens. It is there where she found her love for music. Being born into a family composed of musicians, her grandfather playing drums and father writing music and playing multiple instruments, Olivia has grown fond to the art and has become a singer and song writer herself. "I have been singing from the time that I could talk. Although I just began pursuing a music career less than a year ago, I am passionate about it and hope for success." Her vocals are fresh, refined and very enlightening; MELODIC!!! The art of music is something embedded deep within Olivia and has shown itself something fierce lately.

It all started at the young age of 13 doing background vocals for gospel singer Nancey Jackson on the song "A Star", which can be found on the album 'Free (Yes, I'm Free)' released October 7, 1997. Olivia's first solo track was recorded in May of 2011. Olivia writes her own music and she use to play the drums like her grandfather and work a piano. Her musical influences include Ray Charles, Faith Evans, Mary J. Blige, Karen Clarke Sheard, Kim Burrell and Sarah Vaughan, to name a few.

One of Olivia's proudest moments to date was the 'I Love Life' tour with Life Camp Inc.; there she experienced what it was like being able to share her gift with inner city children, prison/jail inmates and those that lost their children due to gun violence. Olivia has also had the chance to share the stage with Russell Simmons, Erica Ford, Slowbucks T and a host of other artists. She has opened up shows for comedians such as Omar Thompson, Freddie Ricks and Talent. Olivia has performed live jazz at Justin's Restaurant at the age of 16, not to mention she recently performed at the National Action Network (Al Sharpton's headquarters) in Harlem NY.

Tracks like "Consider It" and "Love's Door" gives you that tingle that makes you say, "Damn, I'm feeling this!!" Her clear cut voice, open style and determined attitude, makes you want to give her a chance to show the world what she can do. Talk about bringing the 'R' in R&B back, she is definitely the one. She is no doubt what the music industry is missing! Olivia just recently dropped her new single "Over It" in February and will drop an EP this 2012 summer. She will also be featured in an up and coming issue of "X3magazine" as well as performing all over New York City. Currently Olivia is working with

'TAKIF' on the "Achieve Your Dream" tour, which rewards public school students with sneakers, cell phones and more all for academic achievements! If you would like to tune into her music, you can check out her music at www.soundcloud.com/olivia-gilmore.

Currently to date, Olivia released the single 'G Lovin" in the year 2013 and in March of 2014 another hot single titled "Matrix". Olivia is working vigorously on recording an album, but you can tune into Ms. Gilmore's music on a variety of blog sites such as; singersroom.com theNewLoFi.com & youKnowIGotSoul.com. Her music has even been featured on Hypemachine.com radio show while having online publications such as The Hype magazine. Her music has been featured on mixtapes across the US & UK as well as many sold out clubs such as SOBs, BB Kings, Santos Party House & restaurants like the well-known Sugar Bar and many others within in the tri-state area.

Olivia is currently working on a new EP titled "Rise of The Underdog" slated to be released this fall. Give her music a chance and I GUARANTEE you will be satisfied!! BELIEVE THAT!!!

For all business inquiries or to find out more about *Olivia Gilmore* contact info: bookoliviagilmore@gmail.com

TR3

"ELEVATE WITH A YOUTH"

Queens, NY always takes me to another level of understanding, but this time I want to know where has this kid been all this time? John Pritchett aka Tr3 is the youngest artist I have been pleasured to do business with. Born and currently growing up in East Elmhurst, NY, this young man is evolving to a level of Definite Elevation.

Born on December 6, 1999, Tr3 entered the world with ambition and now at the ripe age of 14 he is shocking many with his lyrical skills and impressing the young ladies with his charm. His inspiration for music comes from the feeling of writing songs and being able to express how he feels and most importantly, being able to escape from all that is currently going on while he writes. He says that fame is also his inspiration he wants to be the "person whom is seen frequently, looked up to and listened to on a daily." With that said, I back Tr3 up a 100% and then some because he has awed me that much.

My first sighting of this youngster was on KSHARK TV Queens cypher and if I must say, Tr3 should have been saved for last because you know what they say, if you don't believe me, you'll have to see for yourself.

Tr3 is so young I had to inquire on where he planned on being within the next 5 years and his smooth response was just as so, "I see myself probably getting more known than I currently am drastically, getting a record deal contract and still making music and exploring other careers. Awards, Albums, Fortune, Fame, that's basically what I see coming in my next 5 years." An optimistic outlook on his life, I'm digging this kid!!

With all that we have taken in thus far, what would make anyone recognize you as an artist, what makes you standout? Tr3 with his bright smile and confident posture responded, "I try my best to tell the truth of my stories and the realism of the outside world while still using a good vocabulary, catchy and clever punch lines and amazing literary devices, (similes, metaphors, etc.) which we don't hear on the radio that much. Plus I'm still at a young age and I'm only getting better as time progresses, so I can only imagine how it will be for me as I grow older. I distance myself from the music within and circling my age group, therefore, I believe I have what it takes to compete with artist you see and hear in the media now, even the legends of the game."

In contrast or comparison to other main stream artists I would have to go with whom Tr3 would say he can compare to in distinct ways and that person is Nas. If you have not heard this kid in the KSHARK TV Cypher out of Queens, East Elmhurst, then you might want to take a listen because his skills were impressing for a young 14 year old kid!

What impresses me the most about Tr3 is the fact that his work is phenomenal beyond his age limit. Prime example to my belief is his latest track title 'Do Ya Like' emphasizing his thoughts and emotions on his recent breakup, but by no means has the youngster let it get the best of him. He is persistently working on his album and has focused on creating a brand for himself, focused and determined, my kind of guy!!

Tr3's work to date; a 10 song EP titled "Hurst Finest" which can be found on hotnewhiphop.com and a new mixtape entitled "D.I.M.E (Dedication, Inspiration, Motivation, Elevation)". His accomplishments thus far; "I'm a two time Floetry (Rap + Poetry) Competition winner at PS 127, and I also had a poem published into the American Library of Poetry 2008 Edition Book", Young John 'Tr3' Pritchett announced firmly and proud.

We will keep checking up on Tr3 for all his latest work and projects so stay tuned in, BELIEVE DAT!!!

Artist of the Summer
BILLY BANG
RARE BREED

"Everything is rhythm, the way we walk, the way we

Queens has bred many well-known individuals and has lost just as many, but I've been privileged to work with a rare and unique artist ready to take over the map. This artist has earned some well-deserved stripes in the field of entertainment and I'm obliged to be working with him.

Prafit aka Billy BANG, was raised in the town of Lefrak City, born January 26th, 1987 to a hood Legend, the Original Billy Bang and his mom. This young man has transmogrified from a "bad boy" to an extraordinary college graduate. He has mastered the art of music in as little as 10 years. He successfully completed college (Howard University) with a Bachelor's Degree in Radio/TV/Film with a concentration in Audio Production.

Growing up in the golden years of hip-hop, Billy BANG took in every aspect of the music world by
listening to artists such as Kwame', Salt n Pepa, Rakim and others. He began rapping at 10 years old and although music was his passion, he had other things he occupied his time with. He did voices over Sesame Street and performed in plays as well as participating in sports such as track and football

Although Billy BANG has his heart in the music, if he does not prevail with it he will still continue to do what his heart desires. Music is his passion. Aside from
creating melodies and laying vocals and creating rhymes, Billy BANG has acted in two independent films that he has won an award and trophy for. He has been told that "acting is his calling' because he can emulate or
internalize a role rather than mimic it.

No question, most artists do not look to be compared to anyone and Billy BANG definitely does not, but to
compare him I'd say Tupac is a definite hit, but not as an artist or actor, just simply as an individual with a light in him.
Billy BANG made his 1st appearance featured on SoSo Def recording artist Brandon Hines' 2005 debut album 'Love Music' on the track titled 'We Need We'. Along with that, he has released numerous amounts of solo projects and has appeared on other venues like BET's 'The Deal' as D.C's next up & coming underground artist in May of 2010. Next, the album 'C.R.E.A.M', also released in 2010, doubled as the soundtrack to the independent movie CREAM written and directed by Emmy Award winner Ryan Cole.

talk, the way our hearts beat, music is a part of us"

Then on July 22nd, 2010 a very special day, Billy BANG released another project titled 'REINCARNATED' dedicated to his father whom had passed away while Billy BANG was only 17 years old. While attending college, Billy BANG was voted by student body Howard's Hottest MC in October 2010. He has also made an appearance on DJ Kay Slays' radio show 'SHADE 45'.

I asked Billy BANG why not be a doctor or a lawyer; His response was simply, "he's not in it for the money and so forth. He gets pleasure out of knowing his music can touch someone he does not know. That's the bliss."

In 5 years he hopes to be on, but if that is not so, then he may end up traveling abroad and teaching English in other countries. Sounds odd huh? ..yea, but hey, "not every individual has the same motivations in life."

His worse fear is living and working the 9-5 life style. He doesn't want to be stuck finding a love for new things and growing old to what he set forth to accomplish with music. Currently Billy BANG is working on another project with a track titled 'Alright' and I was privileged to be the 1st to hear the final work and I must say DAMN!!, this kid is amazing!! I usually hear unsigned artist who

this kid is amazing!! I usually hear unsigned artist who all sound alike and speak about the same things, but Billy BANGs' work is unique and has variety to it. Billy BANG has a Cali'- Nate Dogg flow with a mix of that ole school Rakim and Kwame' living in him.

Currently to date Billy BANG has signed with Independent label The Chemist and has featured on the remake of 'Candy Rain' by Anthony Lewis. He also has a track titled 'Kickn Game' and I fell in love with it instantly!!!

Working with this "college boy" is a blessing and a pleasure!! Together he and I will definitely bring back that world of hip-hop that the world is yearning for. Expect a lot to come from Billy BANG because this is only the beginning BELIEVE THAT!!!

STEPH STONE

AVAILABLE ON DATPIFF.COM

HIP HOP ON A COME BACK

Where did Hip-Hop go? What happened to the music we use to love to hear from artist like Nas, Jay-Z, B.I.G and A-Z, just to name a few? In this day and age a lot of the music we once loved has slowly dissipated, but I think I may have found the solution to this problem. Stephon Blakely aka Steph Stone, an unsigned artist has managed to catch my attention with his nostalgic wave of energy in his music. Steph, a native of Jamaica, Queens is slowly making his way to the scene, but in a nonchalant kind of way. He is an artist whom is not trying to get signed by any label, but is simply trying to create a brand and meet the certain demands of the entertainment business. He is an entrepreneur creating a certain entity so that others can just ride to the energy of his music. His goal with this music thing is to create his own lane and ride with it to see where it goes and while in that process, take younger artist under his wing and help to bring them to the next level.

For an individual who has no back support, he has managed to reach 5000 hits on youtube for the video Sunday Service and as you read this, the hits continue. Right now his 1st album is out 'Welcome 2 Tha Stone Age' hosted by DJ ProStyle and he is on his 2nd

What makes Steph different from the other's is knowing that he is not out to become famous, he creates his music not only for our enjoyment but because its what's in him and what helps to express who he is and album release party while working on his next video and album. some of what he has been through. Not to be compared to anyone, but if I can think of someone to compare him to, it would have to be Nas because of the calm flow that he has when telling his "stories". Although his lyrics can be pretty raw, he definitely does not present them in such an aggressive manner. If I can suggest a song for your enjoyment from his album, it would be 'Tha Mary Joint', it's a roll the windows down in the summer, crank up the volume and ride out kind of song.

I suggest you all get to know Steph Stone because he is here to stay and he will surely put a mark in the music industry and bring it back to its frame of nature we were once use to.

CCLASS AVE
"It Chose Me"

Chan Davis was born and raised in Brownsville Brooklyn, the city of The Notorious B.I.G, Jay Z and Foxy Brown to name a few.

CClass stated that music chose him in a sense of being "therapeutic". He loves and adores creating music and cherishes everything about it. "Just being able to vibe with the melodies and hear it all come to life is amazing!" And I must say, I do agree, for music is such a motivator in many different senses. Music speaks volumes when words can't express how one is feeling.

The inspiration of music is the feeling CClass gets when he see's people enjoying his music, dancing and singing to the melody. Sometimes simply listening to other artists, hearing them through the tunnels and channels is a moment of gratitude because it drives him to create more music, thus leading to collaborations. Collaborating with other artists is an idea that strikes many well-known signed and unsigned artists and for CClass, working with Kanye, Jeezy, Nas and a few others like 50 Cent would be a pleasure!!

CClass refers to these individuals as the 'soulful street artists' He does not compare himself to any other artist, but in comparison of creative thoughts, CClass says he falls into line with Jay Z and 50 to only name a few. His reference to the entrepreneurs is that the environment, in which they adapted and acquired their style, is the same element that gives him the motivation he has today.

Many unsigned artists look to bigger ventures if the music career does not flourish and when asked about other endeavors CClass answered that he currently has a clothing line that he had out a few years back that is looking to make rise to the top these coming years. He currently has a mixtape business he wants to reveal to the world and he wants to further his dreams of continuing his artistry as a cartoon animator. CClass seems to have his goals pretty laid out and I hope that all prevails for him.

Currently to date he has a few tracks out that you must listen to, but the 2 that I suggest for your ears are 'G'd Up' remix ft. Fred the Godson and 'Thug Shit' ft. Arlis Michaels & Priceless. CClass is on his way to stardom and I am going to be right alongside this artist to keep up with all his latest work, I suggest you do the same, BELIEVE DAT!!

HOOD Legend
QUEENS EDITION

*The bodies of stories, whether non-historical or unverifiable,
They are passed down from a generation of prior existence to a generation
consumed of popular stories made to be accepted as historic,
Especially when they relate to a particular person –
DEFINITION OF A LEGEND….
William 'Billy BANG' Clark – DEFINITION OF A HOOD LEGEND…*

BILLY BANG

The era of the late 70's, - where music was taken aback by the voices of The Temptations and many others ushered in a new era of music where the vibe was nothing but MONEY and STREET FAME, the 80's!! William Clark, - deriving the name Billy Bang grew up in the city of Queens in a town called Lefrak City, where most of the infamous hustlers and gamblers dwelled. 'Queens Get the Money' is the slogan known till this day and Lefrak was definitely housing an acceptable amount of those particular 'Get Money' individuals.

As the 80's rolled in, the classics kicked off, - Eric B & Rakim', "Thinking of a Master Plan, cause ain't nothing but sweat inside my hand…" was one of the many tunes ringing through the radios in homes all across NYC. The BMW E30 was the car that was making its mark but that was just until that pretty BMW 315 Convertible made its way into the eyes of just about every hustler there was to name. Without the heavy rope chains that only the true gangsters made popular to the music world along with the pretty ladies to go hand in hand, a gentleman's gentleman

was far from complete. The thick gold bracelets, Rolex watches and Kangoos, either furred out or simple suede, were just the beginning of defining the look of the Original Gangsters. If not an Adidas suit from top to bottom, then you can believe the G's had on the custom made Dapper Dan outfits, - Whether they be Gucci, Louis Vuitton or MCM, - you can guarantee an 'Official Nigga' had them on!!

Don't be alarmed when the finest and "baddest" ladies of the 80's stepped out onto the scene as well decked out in their fur Kangoos with "bamboo earrings, at least two pair, a Fendi bag and a bad attitude!!". And of course their hair stayed on point as always in finger waves or rocking a fresh 1/3 Cesar cut with the curls dropping to the other side, - You could NEVER say the 80's wasn't the decade to remember!!

It takes a lot of credential and attributes to be considered a 'Legend', let alone a 'Hood Legend'. It is not just stories combined and tales of the unknown that formulate a person to be who they are, it is that person alone that will create the perception people around them will either grow to love or hate. William Clark known to everyone as the Original Billy Bang from Lefrak City, Queens, where he was born and raised, was one of the all-time favorite hustlers' hustler and ladies' man. Although he gained his notoriety from countless run-ins with the law and a few street rivals, he was still a very well-respected individual with a lot of charm and intelligence.

As the 80's spiraled in, so did the drugs and with that came the main frame of life, HUSTLING!! Amongst the many individuals in Lefrak City, only but a few stood out above the rest. Names such as; L.A., Surf, Gremlin Divine, Juda, Bentley and E-Money Bags, to reference a few, were the ones that rang bells throughout not only Lefrak City, - but all five boroughs.

Billy Bang stood at about 6" tall and was well-built and fit from being incarcerated numerous times. He was a handsome, light skinned fella with a smile that magnetized

people and enchanted the women. Billy was known for his stick-up ways and get-money schemes that, although at the time made for a lavish lifestyle, were the rising of his downfall.

 When it comes to music, what song can you say reminded you of Billy? I asked Fahyed, close friend of Billy Bang growing up and as he laughed smoothly, Fahyed responded, "Keep Rising to The Top" by Keni Burke; then he continued on, "Billy was a good dude, wild, (he gestured with a smile while closing his eyes to reminisce more) but a very cool dude! He spent so much time in and out of prison he was built like a monster and he was very fit. He was a pretty boy who got fly, but he just loved robbing people, that was his thing!" I always wondered whether a person of Billy's stature and demeanor could be loved honestly or hated faithfully, because how can someone viewed to be so ruthless have so many people who loved him?; Impossible, some may think and feel, but truthfully, people are not always what they present themselves to be. Deep inside and behind closed doors, 'villains' turn into 'victors' and reveal who they really are. Billy was indeed a man with an adventuresome way of living, but he was human.

 As a child, no one would have really thought that Billy would become a stick-up kid, but by the time he reached his teens, he had already gained a reputation for shooting and robbing people. Although he had a family who loved him and enormous amount of respect from others, he chose this 'bad boy' lifestyle and I would say it was because of the adrenaline rush a person has in the mêlée of these actions. Billy spent most of his life in and out of prison and during these bids he lost time with his son, who has grown to be a very well-educated and rounded person striving for the best. Yet, each time Billy would return home from these years away in prison, it was as if he had a new action plan toward his stick-up ways and it only progressed to robbing people in the music industry.

 The music scene was becoming the main frame of how people idolized life and how the Real G's perceived it. Movies like 'Scarface' and 'Paid In Full' were the movies hitting the screens and while Al Pacino was making a name for himself, so was William 'Billy Bang' Clark. Billy Bang was deep in the game by this time and his ruthless ways were becoming more volatile.

 As Billy grew in size, his hunger for crime grew intensely as well. I can recall looking at pictures of Billy and seeing a man who was there in person, but in thought, he was somewhere else. "Everything about him was comical, yet serious, he always made us laugh!!" replied his son when asked about his father Billy and not the legend. A man who spoke intelligently and who would assist his grandmother from her car to her door after church was the same man that advertently took the lives of others and stole from top-notch individuals, How can they be of one person? Simple, he was just a person who had a "larger than life aura about himself" says his son, "He stood out in the largest crowds!!"

 Billy's run-ins with rivals and street individuals were becoming more than just a life-style and daily regimen, they were beginning to weigh down on his better judgment and the choices he made.

 By 2004, the music era had transitioned so much it ultimately changed the perceptions of life for many. For Billy Bang everything remained the same until one dreadful December evening.

 Late Sunday night, December 27, 2004, not long after the moon had finally rested itself among the stars, William 'Billy Bang' Clark decided to step outside of the LQ club, which was one of the places to be that evening as it was rap star Ja Rule's eventful party for the holidays. Along with a few associates, Billy congregated amidst the cold, frigid air until unexpectedly, the final hours of his life came crashing down on him. An unidentified man fired multiple shots into the crowd of people standing outside and among those that were hit was Billy Bang. Sadly, the final moments when Billy Bang ran and collapsed were caught in the eyes of a bystander who attempted to help, but was warded off by police, she stated Billy lied there clutching his wounds while trying to preserve life until medical help arrived. 'Timing is of the essence'; Monday afternoon, hours after being admitted into the hospital, William Clark died of his injuries and 'Billy Bang' died due to "wasted talent" but was ultimately 'REINCARNATED' into a Legend. This lifestyle is not to be glorified because there are only two ways to end this way of life if you are not capable of making a change before it is too late. Although Billy was loved by many, he was also disliked by some as well. The eyes that peer in from the outside see lavishness and a high way of living, but no one really takes into account the damage that is being created to one's self and others living such a way. No one sees reality until it hits home, but by then it is too late.

 My articles on 'Hood Legends' are not to praise the life style by any means but to bring to light the fact that we have carelessly lost lives to this same way of life for years. We debate it, yet we idolize it; we encourage our kids to live differently, but yet our children know the lyrics to its songs better than they know the alphabet. It's saddening. William Clark could have been anything or anyone he wanted to be since he was by no means a fool or unintelligent, but he never learned how to channel his biggest and best attributes in a way that brought the light upon himself without demanding too much in return.

 Not to glorify, but to use a dimmed light to strengthen someone else's….. May you continue to Rest in Paradise William 'Billy Bang' Clark….

NIKKI M.

Model & CEO Of Be Your Own Beauty Cosmedics

   Elegance and grace is not something that is easily found now-a-days, but fortunately, I have been privileged time and time again by the presence of these kinds of folk.
   Nicole Mendez, born and raised in Queens, NY has always dreamed big and hoped for that time that she can finally shine as bright as the star that sits high in the sky watching over her. Growing up in a family full of talented and intelligent people, Nicole was blessed to have both parents who believed in her and as her father would always say, "she is a star!!"
   Nicole took the words of her father and allowed her creative side to take charge leading her to a destination she knew she could always reach. "People swear pretty girls always look for a come up, but I made the choice to make my own way and be my own come up!!" Her son being her motivation and her family as her number 1 fan is the reason she has not given up on her dreams and biggest endeavors. After suffering the loss of her best friend, her dad, she chose to push harder so that his spot in the sky would shine even brighter.

   Nicole opted on inspiring women to overcome the difficulties of life and its tribulations by designing her own cosmetic line B,Y.O.B (BE YOUR OWN BEAUTY) that basically says, "You don't have to look how you feel when going through hard times, instead, you can embrace your struggles and wear your strength in the place people see most, your face!!" Along with her cosmetic line Nicole also models in which she has been doing since the age of 22, so if you don't know this young lady, I suggest you get familiar, because like anything in life, things take time to blossom and B.Y.O.B will be the next big thing, BELIEVE DAT!!!

BOOKINGS/INQUIRIES byourownbeauty@gmail.com
INSTAGRAM: @BeYourOwnBeautycosmetics

KIZER
/KSHARK TV

"EVERY DETAIL HAS A PURPOSE IN WHAT WE DO. WE ARE THE ORIGINAL COPY..... THE BLUEPRINT PRESERVING UNDERGROUND HIP HOP"

My first attraction to Jay-Z is his skill to be more than just an entertainer. He has awed the world with his skills as an entrepreneur and impressed many when he bought the Nets basketball team, but when it comes to my 'round the way' guys, Felipe Sin aka Fife (the friend/family) aka Kizer (the artist) is the person that as an unsigned artist has impressed me the most when it comes to skills of transforming from artist to entrepreneur.

Felipe Sin, was born November 6th, 19** "No age needed" he stated when asked about his birthday, but proceeded on letting me know that he was born in Queens, N.Y., in a little town called East Elmhurst. Born into a Hispanic background, father a Priest and mother a development specialist, Felipe embraced the lively hood of growing up amongst mixed cultures in NYC. He grew up in East Elmhurst among friends and family, but attended school in the Bronx from Kindergarten to High school. That small margin could be the reason he has such a love for music!

What is his drive for such a success thus far you might ask and so Felipe replied, *"My pain and life experiences motivate me to do my music or anything related to hip hop... That's my secret weapon lol"* and I must agree that life experiences and pain is what motivates the best artist we have seen in a lifetime. Most of Felipe's work started out as an unsigned artist along with a few close friends forming the group GBH-Ghotta Be Hood.

Eventually GBH's hard work as individuals led them to the next level of entrepreneurship thus leading to the idea and creation of 'KSHARK TV' a small broadcasting of unsigned artists performing in cyphers for a few moments of fame and I must say, what an incredible job Felipe has done with this project, I am honored to know such and enthusiastic and hard-working person.

Who intrigues you the most as far as working with, artist wise, then as an owner of a prestigious and growing business, whom would you work with being that you have worked with artists such as Chris Rivers (Big Pun's Son), 40 Cal, & Papoose to name a few?

" As far as an artist I would love to work with Kanye West. The man is a genus whether you like his music or not. As a CEO of KsharkTV, I would like to work with people like Sergio Parra from Square Deal Media."KSHARK TV", where did this idea originate? I asked.

Felipe's response was interesting, while in the group GBH and being signed to a few deals but never getting past the underground mark, Felipe came up with the concept of KSAHRK TV , "I felt no one really was doing much to help groups and artist like myself get the exposure they needed." That concept and idea was the best thing that has happened to Kizer and his team.

Other online websites such as VLAD TV, FORBEZDVD, WSHH and 50 cents THISIS50.com have taken on the opportunity of posting a few of the most liked cyphers to date, so if you have no clue of what's going on, you can easily catch up and I suggest you do. This young man has proven he can break barriers and strive for a better purpose so check him out as well as his work

Candice Jay

Here comes the most abrupt question, what if music dose not thrive for you, what do you do? Well, Candice Jay had a very eloquent reply and it was simply that she does not concentrate on the after, she is living for now, but she does have a few other things brewing in which she can aspire to pursue during her music career or after. Candice Jay is an entrepreneur so her next project will be working on owning her own company. For now, Candice is focused on the whims of now and creating a brand and a wave to ride that will take you to a place you've never thought music could take you to.

A 'MAGNETIC ESSENCE' is the phrase Miss Candice Jay uses when describing her aura and the vibe she allures her fans with. I must say I agree because of her particular choice of music for a young woman entering the music industry. I have to say though, I am intrigued by her choice of melody and tunes because it is different and what makes Candice Jay stand out. If you want to hear some of what she has accomplished to date, check her out on youtube.com/CandiceJayMusic, trust me you will not be disappointed. Look out for her upcoming music as well!!!

What I adore most is an original artist coming from their own brand, cut from their own cloth. Candice Johnson known to the entertainment world as Candice Jay born April 1st in the loving 80's, is an inspiring R&B artist going through the realms of creating her own style.

Candice Jay wants to be known for her eccentric and alternative style of music. Candice Jay's inspirations for music, one thing, life!! "Everything I encounter is a story and experience that someone is going through and needs to be heard." is what Candice Jay replied when asked what in life draws her to creating sounds and melodies. She also stated that she has always had a yearning and passion for the art itself and it will NEVER go away!!

Currently Candice Jay is working her first EP that is untitled as of the moment. She is striving on marketing herself and working on going viral with all of her up and coming success. Candice Jay has performed at a few venues and her performances I must say were awesome!! Her voice is beautiful and the very fact that she has a different style of music is what makes her stand out from the rest.

In the years to come Candice Jay wants to be able to enjoy the fruits of her labor while creating and performing full time. When asked who she most considers working with she answered, "There are so many great artist but I would love to create a project with Justin Timberlake." I do concur because I believe these two artist voices' together would be phenomenal!!

Certified Loyal & Sincerely Honest

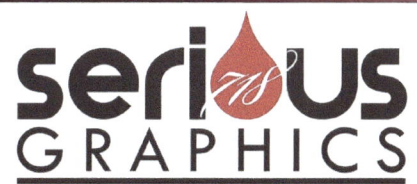

Bernard Granum II
Graphic Designer/Photographer
CEO Serious Graphics 718

Graphic designers come a dime a dozen, but you won't find many graphic designers with the art of advertising and marketing as well. Luckily I was honored to meet Mr. Bernard Granum II, the CEO and founder of 'Serious Graphics 718' based out of Jamaica, Queens.

Bernard, a well-rounded individual, spends most his time designing and implementing marketing promotions for businesses creating logos, letterheads, business cards, flyers and more. He specializes in corporate identity design, print design and branding. His talent speaks for itself and his work is phenomenal!!

With over 14 years of experience, Bernard is looking to expand his brand to a wider audience so if you are looking for a dedicated graphic designer, feel free to get in contact with Mr. Granum via email at seriousndpgfx@gmail.com. If you want to view his work, follow him on Instagram and Facebook as well. Get familiar with this self-proclaimed business man because he is making foot-prints in the sand, follow him, BELIEVE DAT!!

DESIGN SERVICES
- LOGO DESIGNS
- BROCHURES
- CD/DVD COVER ART & INSERTS
- FLYERS
- POSTERS
- ADVERTISEMENTS
- WEB BANNERS
- BANNERS
- BILLBOARDS
- MAGAZINE ADS
- FULL MAGAZINES
- AND MORE

PROGRAMS
- ADOBE ILLUSTRATOR CS/CC
- ADOBE PHOTOSHOP CS/CC
- ADOBE INDESIGN CS/CS6

MORE SERVICES
- VIDEO EDITING
- MUSIC PRODUCTION
- PHOTOGRAPHY
- VIDEO RECORDING

WWW.NDPKING.WIX.COM/SERIOUSGRAPHICS
INSTAGRAM: SERIOUSNDPGFX | FACEBOOK.COM/SERIOUSGRAPHICS718

www.ingramcontent.com/pod-product-compliance
Lightning Source LLC
Chambersburg PA
CBHW041234040426
42444CB00002B/157